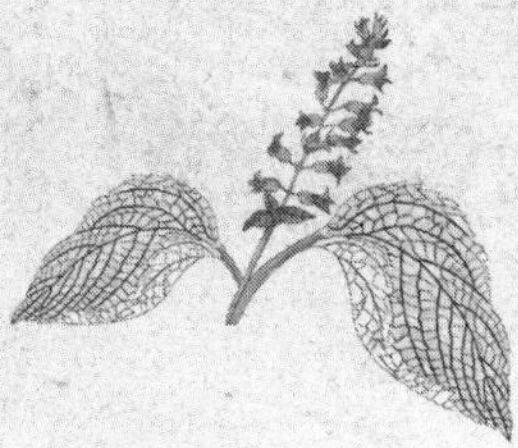

This book belongs to ....

....